Unprecedented
Press

The Best Kids Explore Arizona © 2022 by Joshua Best

All rights reserved. No part of this publication may be reproduced, distributed, or transmitted in any form or by any means, including photocopying, recording, or other electronic or mechanical methods, without the prior written permission of the publisher or author, except in the case of brief quotations embodied in critical reviews and certain other noncommercial uses permitted by copyright law. For permission requests, email the publisher or author at addresses below:

Contact the publisher:
Unprecedented Press LLC - 229 W Main Ave, Zeeland, MI 49464
www.unprecedentedpress.com | info@unprecedentedpress.com
instagram: unprecedentedpress

ISBN: 979-8-9867126-0-4

Ingram Printing & Distribution, 2022

First Edition

the BEST KIDS explore

FEATURING: maps, reviews, travel tips, and true tales of family adventures

ARIZONA

An illustrated, story-driven travel guide for kids

CONTENTS

MEET THE KIDS 4
LODGING & TRANSPORT 6
STORIES:

OASIS IN THE DESERT 8
in Scottsdale, AZ

BERRY WELL 16
in Tortilla Flat, AZ

FAST FRIENDS 22
in Gilbert, AZ

ANIMAL STYLE 28
in Phoenix, AZ

RELUCTANT FLYERS 36
in Mesa, AZ

LITTLE DETAILS 42
BEST BETS 43
BUMPS IN THE ROAD 44
BEST BITES 45

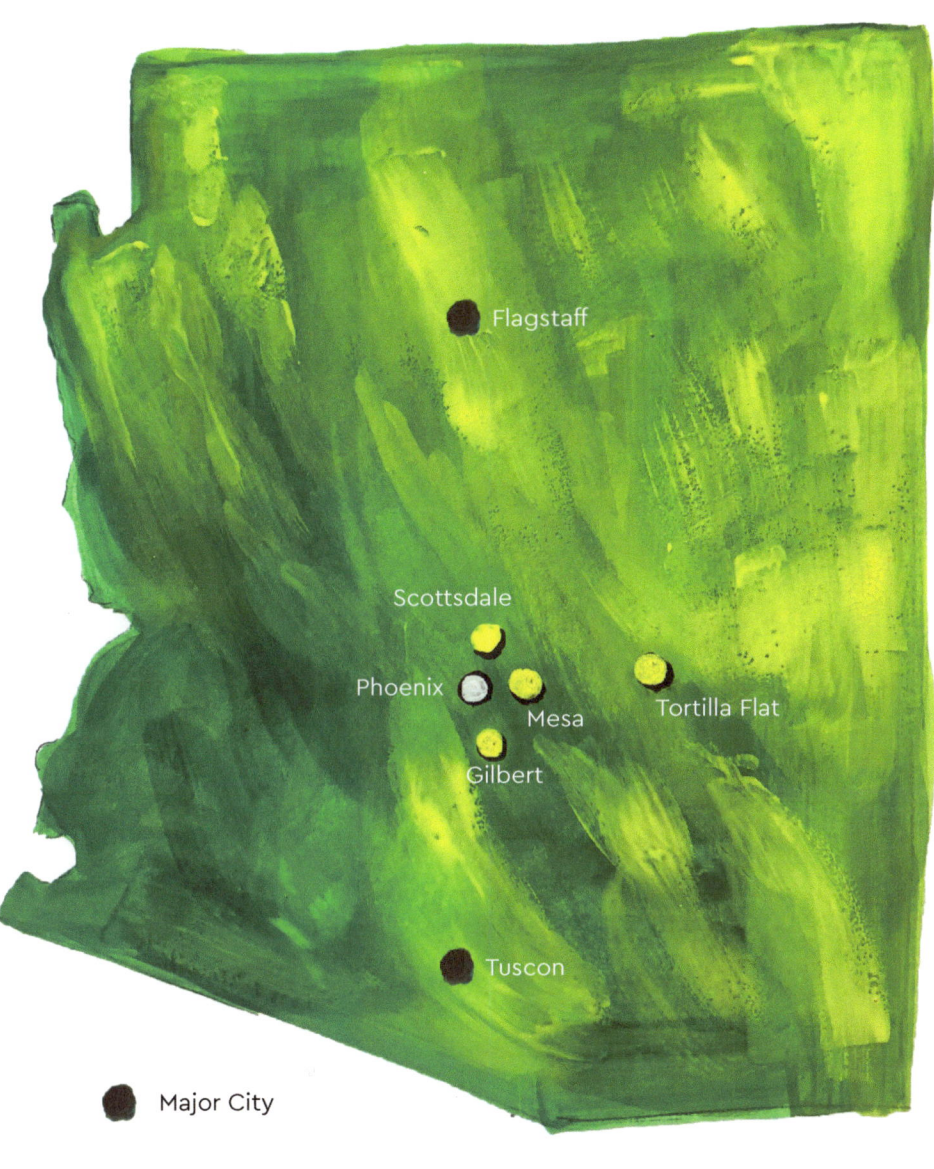

MEET THE KIDS

Exploring is the best. Exploring lets you discover the cool things around you – things you didn't know were there before. That's what makes it so much fun! It's exciting to find out what's around the corner, across the border and beyond the horizon.

The Best kids are explorers. They love finding new places to play and discovering new ways to have fun. The oldest is Frederick – he has orange hair. The middle child is Edith – she has brown hair. The youngest is Hugo – he has yellow hair. The Best kids are half American and half Canadian. They live in Michigan.

In this book, the kids travel to the state of Arizona. At the time of their expedition, Frederick was seven years old, Edith was five years old, and Hugo was two years old. This trip occurred in the month of February.

LODGING & TRANSPORT

The Best family travelled to Arizona by airplane. They flew into Mesa Gateway Airport on Allegiant Air. The flights were very affordable, and took roughly three and a half hours.

To explore the region, the Bests rented a car. After waiting in the line up for a very long time, they were eventually paired with a white Toyota Camry.

RESIDENCE INN MESA EAST

For lodging, the kids stayed in a hotel called Residence Inn on the eastern edge of Mesa. It was newly built (still being landscaped), and very clean. Their room had a kitchen and a bedroom with a door so they could go to bed one at a time.

Conveniently, there was a Sprouts grocery store nearby, a swimming pool on the property, and a beautiful view of the mountains. The kids were very happy with the hotel breakfast each morning.

OASIS IN THE DESERT

On a cold February morning, the Best kids rose out of bed before the sun rose in the sky.

It was the morning after Valentine's Day, and the Best kids we're flying to the great state of Arizona. With their bags all packed, they were getting excited to explore the desert, but Frederick (the family's resident philosopher) had some doubts. He wasn't sure the Phoenix area could live up to the Orlando trip they took the previous year. While discussing their travel plans, he was once heard saying,

"Yeah… Arizona might be pretty good. Maybe."

With that level of optimism, the kids piled into the car. Hugo and Edith were half asleep, but once they arrived at the airport, even Frederick perked up and was ready to fly across the country. Much to their disappointment, the airport was extremely busy. It seemed as if every person in Michigan had come to the airport at the exact same time. To check their bags, they waited in a lineup that curved around the entire airport like a string. Then, they waited to pass through security in a line that weaved back-and-forth like a snake.

By the time the Best family arrived at their airport gate, they discovered that everyone else had already boarded the aircraft. They got on the airplane just minutes before the door closed! As they sat in their seats, they breathed a sigh of relief, and the jet engine lifted them up – away from all the chaos. As they passed through a ceiling of clouds, Edith (who was in the window seat) got everyone's attention, "Look! I can see the sun coming up!"

The flight was three hours long, crossed two time zones, and flew in the opposite direction of the rising sun. The plane landed in Arizona at just 8:30 in the morning, but the hotel check-in wasn't until 3 p.m.!

After retrieving their bags and their rental car, they decided to go for a second breakfast, and start exploring the area. They first took the obligatory drive up South Mountain Road. On the way up, the kids (and their mom) fell asleep while listening to a Harry Potter audiobook. They woke up and discovered an amazing view of Phoenix at Dobbins Lookout. Now it was 12 p.m. and they needed another activity.

The agreement (needed to avoid arguments) was to allow each person in the family to select an excursion on the trip. In an effort to curb a chaotic morning, they let their mom pick first. Everyone guessed she would pick the Desert Botanical Garden near Scottsdale and they were right.

Driving onto the facility was an incredible experience. The gardens are surrounded by Papago Park's rugged rocks and hardy shrubs. The first thing the kids saw was an installation of colorful lemurs amid the bunches of exotic desert plants. As they entered past the ticket booth, they realized the entire grounds were peppered with gigantic animal sculptures made of bright orange, green, pink and blue plastic. They were an incredible sight to see and they made the gardens more fun for kids.

The Best crew continued to walk along the path, and spotted some incredible desert plants. Some were sharp and spiky, others were vibrant and beautiful. At one point, Hugo was chased by a bee that was collecting pollen from a patch of purple wildflowers. He held it together, but the bee gave him quite a fright.

Toward the end of the experience, they stumbled upon a reflection pool. The area was so peaceful. It felt like an oasis. Not just an oasis from the hot desert sun, but an oasis from the hustle and bustle of daily life in Michigan.

At the reflection pond, there was no homework to do, no toys to clean up, and no chores to tackle. There was just a warm sun, peaceful water, and a tiny hummingbird who came over to say hi. Her wings were fluttering so fast you couldn't even see them, and yet,

she seemed to glide over the glass-like water without a care in the world. It was the perfect remedy for a stressful journey.

Finally, it was 3 p.m. – time for the Bests to check in to their hotel in Mesa.

BERRY WELL

When the Best kids went to Arizona, the seasonal flu was especially strong. Edith and the kids' mom had a nasty bug just one week prior, so they were both sucking Elderberry Lozenges to boost their immune systems. The lozenges were much tastier than typical vitamins and they were careful to take them daily – they were desperate to push past the illness of the previous week.

A couple days into the trip, it was their dad's turn to choose the activity. His choice was the Apache Trail, a rural road that took them through the Superstition Mountains. Along the route, the kids stopped for excursions at Lost Dutchman State Park, where they hiked a desert

trail, and Goldfield Ghost Town, an old western mine area where they shot bright blue toy rifles at targets to win a prize.

The road was steep and curvy with incredible vistas. Along the Apache Trail, there are forests of Saguaro Cacti – an amazing sight. It looked like the setting from Looney Tunes where Wile E. Coyote tries to catch the Road Runner.

At the end of their journey, they came to a tiny town in the middle of nowhere called Tortilla Flat. It was a small tourist stop with a one room museum, a post office, a restaurant and an ice cream shop.

"Can we get ice cream???" Hugo asked.

Their parents agreed, but first they needed lunch. The Best kids filed into the local tavern where the walls were decorated with dollar bills and the bathrooms were laden with paintings of cartoon cowboys and cowgirls. The nachos they ordered weren't great, but the decor was very memorable.

After dinner, the kids ran quickly down the old, wooden boardwalk to the ice cream shop. They served all the regular flavors like chocolate and mint chip, but the kids' dad spotted a flavor that was pretty unique – Prickly Pear, a pink ice cream that comes from the fruit of a Prickly Pear cactus. He dared the kids to try it. Frederick took him up on it.

The Bests sat down on a weather-worn wooden log by

the parking lot. Together, they enjoyed their cones in the sunshine. Without much success, they tried to lick the melting ice cream that was cascading down their fingers. In this moment, they knew the elderberry was working because they were feeling healthy and happy to have traded berry lozenges for Prickly Pear ice cream.

FAST FRIENDS

The Best Kids love hotels for two reasons: the pool and the free breakfast. And what they love most about the free breakfast is the waffles. Hotel waffle makers are somehow the best thing on the planet, so the Best kids decided they would indulge in a waffle every morning of

their vacation in Arizona. Fighting their desire for waffles seemed to go against the spirit of vacation, so their parents were happy to oblige. After just a few mornings, some elderly couples noticed the routine and started taunting the kids to add more toppings.

Hugo didn't know how to react to the goofy seniors, but Frederick and Edith started looking forward to seeing their new buddies every morning at the breakfast buffet.

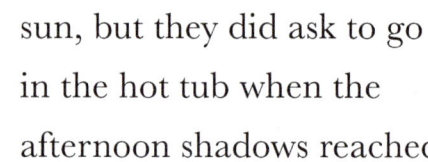

After breakfast, the Best family went to the Legoland Discovery Center. It was filled with rides and activity zones. They even got to see a 4D movie. What's 4D you ask? It's a 3D movie where you get sprayed with water. It was a blast! They also made it to the Children's Museum of Phoenix where they got crazy with paint, navigated a foam maze, and crawled into a giant mushroom.

Later that afternoon, Hugo napped while Frederick and Edith swam in the pool. Jumping and holding their breath underwater didn't get old in the winter sun, but they did ask to go in the hot tub when the afternoon shadows reached

the pool deck. It was the first time the hot tub rules allowed them to go in the bubbling water – they just needed an adult with them. The warm jets felt great – perfect for a cool afternoon.

The Best Kids were certainly enjoying each other's company, but it didn't stop them from missing their friends from back home. That's why Frederick asked if he could call his friend Ezra from the hotel phone when he got back to the room. His parents thought it would be good for him to learn how to use a landline and helped him find Ezra's phone number. Hearing the two talk brought a smile to everyone's face. It was nice to reconnect with someone from back home.

Later that day, when the crew was hungry for dinner, they travelled to Gilbert to find some chow. After checking wait times at a few locations, and realizing most places were full, they landed on a walk-up burrito shop called Topo where they shared a few burritos and bottles of Topo Chico sparkling water. The burritos were delicious, but super spicy. To distract them from their burning tastebuds, they explored the outdoor eating area which was equipped with rope swings, soccer nets on a bright

green turf, and a giant twister board painted on the patio.

"Push me dad!" yelled Hugo as he ran toward the hammock-style swing.

Meanwhile, Edith joined a game of Twister, and Frederick joined a game of soccer with some boys his age. It didn't matter that they didn't know each other. They just introduced themselves, and asked if they could join in. The other kids were happy to have more players! It also didn't matter that they were all from different places, families and cultures. They all played and laughed together for about twenty minutes, then high-fived and waved goodbye.

ANIMAL STYLE

When it was Hugo's turn to pick the attraction, he immediately chose the Phoenix Zoo, which sits close to the Desert Botanical Gardens. Widely known as one of America's great zoos, this destination was a solid hit with the Best kids. Upon entering through the gates, the first thing the kids noticed were more giant animal statues scattered throughout the zoo, but this time they were made of metallic bronze. There was a giant turtle, a crocodile, and a sleek tiger. Without hesitation, they bolted toward the statues and climbed on top of them. After all, what's a zoo without climbable wildlife?

From the main entrance, they received a map and planned their route. First stop? Africa. They started walking, curved to the right and there they were – the elephants. In a large, expensive pen with ropes, tires

and barrels placed around a pond, the elephants played and put on a show. Two-year-old Hugo sat on his dad's shoulders and laughed as the playful creatures blew water out of their trunks.

As the kids continued exploring the zoo, they came across all kinds of animals like flamingos, toucans, and anteaters. Behind a long glass wall, there was even a small family of orangutans. There was a mom (who seemed to be the responsible one), there was a dad (who was quite serious), and there was a little guy (who loved having fun). As the Best kids stood behind the glass, watching the young orangutan, they laughed and pointed at his silly antics. The cute, little guy was jumping all around, throwing his food, and pestering his dad. He also had a red blanket which was his favorite thing to play with. Sometimes he would whip it

around, and other times he placed it on top of his head, while walking around and bumping into things. While Edith and Frederick were giggling, Hugo saw himself in the little orangutan because he too had a special blanket that he took around everywhere.

> **ON PHOENIX ZOO:**
> *"The baby monkey was super funny!"*

Before leaving the zoo, each of the kids picked out a souvenir from the gift shop. Hugo chose to buy a key chain, Edith picked out a necklace with a bear on it, and Frederick walked away with a plush orangutan that looked exactly like the one we watched goof around.

The Best family left the zoo in the late afternoon with sore feet and empty stomachs. They were very hungry! They needed to get dinner fast, so they decided to visit In-N-Out Burger, which can only be found in the western states of the U.S. Visiting In-N-Out was on their to do list, so it was an easy decision.

When they arrived, they approached the counter to order their food, and their dad asked a strange question.

"Who wants to have their hamburger *animal style*?"

The kids looked at each other with confused faces.

"What does that mean?" asked Edith.

Their dad told them it was a secret recipe that isn't listed on the menu. At In-N-Out, asking for *animal style* means they cook your hamburger patty in mustard, they top it with sautéed onions, extra pickles, and they add a special sauce. If you think that's wild, you're not wrong!

Feeling pretty daring, the kids agreed to give *animal style* a try. Soon after, their food was ready.

"Order 49!" shouted the team member. The Best crew gathered their food and found a table on the patio. After a full day of walking around, the food was a perfect treat; it hit the spot. Not only were the *animal style* hamburgers delicious (and messy), they seemed to bring out everyone's fun side. In fact, the Best family laughed and goofed around like the orangutans at the zoo.

RELUCTANT FLYERS

On the last day of their adventure, the Best kids went to the farmers market at a local park in Mesa called Pioneer Park. It was a small, quiet market, but the park was big. More importantly, it was home to the biggest playground they'd ever seen. This playground wasn't twice the size of the average park playground or even three times the size of a normal playground. No, this playground was five or six times bigger than most playgrounds. At the center of it stood a five-story enclosed slide.

In addition to the stellar climbing equipment, the park was also filled with some enormous palm trees and a flock of pigeons that acted like they owned the place.

On the way across the park to the bathroom, Hugo spotted the pigeons. Every time he came upon one, he would yell out, "Pigeon! Pigeon!" and he would run straight toward them. Typically, when a child runs directly at a bird, it flies away. But not these pigeons! They weren't phased by Hugo's sudden approach. No, they simply skipped along on their little legs as if two-year-olds chase them around the park every single day of their lives. The look of Hugo blundering after them, and the unimpressed look on their faces couldn't have been more hilarious!

After climbing, running and playing their hearts out, the Bests packed up their hotel room, and headed for the Mesa airport.

In comparison to Phoenix's Sky Harbor Airport, Mesa's Gateway airport was smaller, but it was also less busy. When they arrived a week prior, they hadn't noticed anything terribly unique about the facility. This time, however, they were three hours early for their flight. After cruising through security, they were left with time to explore.

First, they found the gate, and then they looked around for lunch. They ordered sandwiches and french fries from a pub nearby, but instead of eating the food there, they spotted a sign for a courtyard. The kids' mom was intrigued, so she scouted it out, and what did she find? A pristine desert courtyard featuring large cacti and some other local flora. It was beautiful and sunny,

and it was enormous! Not only were they able to eat outside in the sun, they were also able to walk around on the courtyard path to get some exercise. It was the perfect place to spend their remaining hours. Now they understood why the pigeons wouldn't fly away. This place was too beautiful! The sunshine didn't just warm their bodies, it warmed their hearts.

LITTLE DETAILS

PRICKLY PEAR

The Best kids were happy to try Prickly Pear flavored ice cream, but also a number of other items including Prickly Pear candy, and jam on their morning toast.

WAFFLES

Hotel waffles are always in season! You might think that waffles every morning would be enough for the best kids, but no. They also indulged in waffles at a yummy breakfast restaurant in Gilbert called *The Farmhouse*.

RUG ART

One destination not mentioned in the stories was the Mesa Arts Center. The Best family was able to catch a live Jazz concert there, and then explore the art gallery. A highlight of the gallery was a series of woven rugs designed by artist Morris David Dorenfeld called Color is King: The Hunter Orange Series.

BEST BETS

DESERT BOTANICAL GARDEN

The kids were skeptical at first, but everyone loved the Desert Botanical Garden in Scottsdale. It's a real breath of fresh air.

PHOENIX CHILDREN'S MUSEUM

The children's museum in Phoenix is a really special place. They work really hard to exercise kids' imaginations.

LOST DUTCHMAN STATE PARK

Our simple 1.5 mile hike at this state park was stunning. Positioned in the shadow of the supersition mountains, it's an easy way to make your trip a little more *wild*.

BUMPS IN THE ROAD

LONG DISTANCE PHONE CALL

Frederick's phone call to his friend back in Michigan was a bright spot for him, but we as we checked out of the hotel, we discovered that long distance rates are still a thing on landlines. The bill was *forty dollars*!

WAITING TO CHECK IN

One huge hurdle on this trip was the airport crowds when we departed for Arizona. Not only was their a huge mass of people at the airport, it was also under construction!

BEST BITES

TOPO

This walk-up burrito shop was really fun, and the outdoor seating area was a hit. Unfortunately, the burritos were a little too spicy for the kids.

PIZZERIA BIANCO

With an endorsement from Oprah, we graced this fine establishment. The pizza was thin and delicious. The elevated take on this classic family food made the kids and parents happy.

IN-N-OUT

We make it a habit to visit In-N-Out while out west. It's a fun spot with yummy, but simple fast food. A real classic!

ABOUT THE AUTHOR

The adventures of the Best kids found on these pages were chronicled by none other than their own father. Joshua Best is a writer, designer, and illustrator. By day, he leads the marketing team at a nonprofit network of children's hospitals. Of all these roles, there is none better than being a dad to Frederick, Edith and Hugo.

FOLLOW ALONG

Why wait until the next book is released when you can find out now where the kids are headed? Follow the kids on Instagram to watch illustration in progress and to see real photos of current trips! Also, check out the website for ways to get in touch.

@thebestkids_explore

@thebestkids_explore

thebestkidsexplore.com

www.ingramcontent.com/pod-product-compliance
Lightning Source LLC
Chambersburg PA
CBHW042054060526
44119CB00115B/292